GW00373136

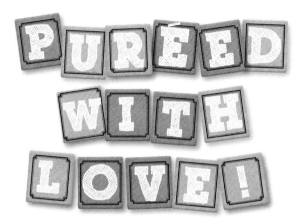

PURÉED WITH LOVE!

Over 75 wholesome baby purée recipes

LOVE FOOD™

First published in 2013
LOVE FOOD is an imprint of Parragon Books Ltd

Parragon
Chartist House
15–17 Trim Street
Bath, BA1 1HA, UK

Copyright © Parragon Books Ltd 2013

LOVE FOOD and the accompanying heart device is a registered trade mark of Parragon Books Ltd
in Australia, the UK, USA, India and the EU.

www.parragon.com/lovefood

ISBN: 978-1-4723-1105-4

Printed in China

Recipes by Rachel Carter
Introduction and nutritional advice by Fiona Hunter
Internal photography by Sian Irvine
Internal food styling by Korrie Bennett

Notes for the Reader

This book uses both metric and imperial measurements. Follow the same units of measurement
throughout; do not mix metric and imperial. All spoon measurements are level: teaspoons are
assumed to be 5 ml, and tablespoons are assumed to be 15 ml. Unless otherwise stated, milk is
assumed to be full fat, eggs and individual vegetables are medium, and pepper is freshly ground
black pepper. Unless otherwise stated, all root vegetables should be washed in plain water and
peeled prior to using.

For best results, use a food thermometer when cooking meat and poultry – check the latest
government guidelines for current advice.

Garnishes, decorations and serving suggestions are all optional and not necessarily included
in the recipe ingredients or method.

The times given are an approximate guide only. Preparation times differ according to the
techniques used by different people and the cooking times may also vary from those given.
Optional ingredients, variations or serving suggestions have not been included in the time
calculations.

Recipes using raw or very lightly cooked eggs should be avoided by infants, the elderly, pregnant
women, convalescents and anyone suffering from an illness. Pregnant and breastfeeding women
are advised to avoid eating peanuts and peanut products. Sufferers from nut allergies should be
aware that some of the ready-made ingredients used in the recipes in this book may contain nuts.
Always check the packaging before use.

Picture acknowledgements

Front cover image: Baby food puréed in saucepan © Dorling Kindersley/Getty Images

contents

introduction

Weaning is an important milestone in your baby's development and an exciting time for both you and your little one. Good nutrition is essential for healthy growth and development and what a child eats in infancy and childhood can have a lasting effect on their health. As a parent, you play an important role in teaching your child to enjoy a wide range of foods and helping to establish good eating habits for life.

Whether you choose to use home-made or shop-bought baby foods depends entirely on your personal preference and circumstances – many parents use a combination of both. Commercial baby foods can certainly be convenient, especially when travelling, so it's useful to have a few jars or packets in the cupboard. However, contrary to popular belief, preparing your baby's food yourself doesn't have to take a lot of time or be a major effort, especially if you cook in batches and freeze the leftovers for another day. It also offers a number of advantages.

Firstly, and perhaps top of the list, is the fact that you have full control over everything your baby eats – you will know exactly what has gone into their food and can ensure that it is fresh, nutritious and free from any additives.

You can also introduce a greater variety of food into your baby's diet than if you were relying on the flavours and ingredients chosen by manufacturers (for example, you're unlikely to find fruit and vegetables like melons, aubergines or avocados in many commercial baby foods).

Making your own baby purées is also a very economical way of feeding your baby – something that cash-strapped families are sure to appreciate! It is also the best way to get them used to eating family food when they are older as the tastes and textures will be familiar.

weaning your baby

Weaning is the gradual process that begins when you start to introduce solid foods into your baby's diet. At around the age of 6 months, milk alone cannot satisfy all your baby's nutritional needs. Their stores of nutrients, such as iron, start to run out and need to be supplemented by a more varied diet. Moving on to more solid foods also helps to develop the muscles necessary for chewing and, eventually, for speech.

The best age to begin weaning is around 6 months, but the exact age depends entirely on the individual baby. Every baby is different and what suits one baby isn't necessarily right for another. There is no advantage in weaning a baby earlier than necessary. In fact, there are several good reasons why the early introduction of solids is not a good idea. Before the age of 4 months, your baby's digestive system may not have developed sufficiently to allow them to cope with foods other than breast or formula milk. Early weaning may also increase the risk of food allergy because the digestive system is not yet fully developed at this age.

How will you know when the time is right?

If your baby still seems hungry after a good milk feed, or wants to feed more frequently than usual, it is often a sign that they are ready for solids. If you are in any doubt, discuss the matter with your health visitor.

During the early stages of weaning, purées are given in addition to the normal quantity of breast or bottle feeds, but as your baby starts to eat larger amounts you can gradually cut down on the milk feeds. However, your baby will continue to need to drink 600 ml/1 pint a day of breast milk, infant formula, follow-on milk (from 6 months) or cow's milk (from 12 months) until around the age of 5.

Weaning stages

The recipes in this book are all suitable from 6 months onwards. However, it is advisable to try single fruit or vegetable purées before introducing those made from a combination of ingredients. The following guidelines are intended as a rough guide – all babies will reach the different stages in their own time.

Stage 1: around 6 months

The first foods introduced should be puréed or sieved to give a thin, smooth consistency, just slightly thicker than milk.

• Start by offering a small amount (about 1–2 teaspoons) of puréed or sieved foods, once a day. You can gradually increase the amount and the frequency.

• Introduce one new food at a time and continue with this food for two or three consecutive days so that you can monitor any reaction.

• Be aware that you may need to offer the same food several times before your baby accepts it.

• Choose a time of the day when you are relaxed and have time to spare. Start by offering some milk and stop part-way through the milk feed to try solids.

try
• Starchy foods (e.g. baby rice mixed with expressed breast or formula milk; cooked, mashed or sieved potato)
• Sieved or puréed fruit (e.g. stewed apple or pear; mango; mashed banana)
• Sieved or puréed cooked vegetables (e.g. carrot; cauliflower; sweet potato; swede; parsnip)
• Well-mashed avocado

Stage 2: after a couple of weeks

You can now start to introduce foods with a thicker consistency and lumpier texture. Increase the variety of foods offered and start to combine foods.

• About now your child should be ready to take fluids from a feeder cup or beaker with a lid. Start by introducing a cup or beaker at one meal.

• Start to introduce finger foods (see opposite page) as soon as your baby shows interest.

• During feeding, always make sure your baby is strapped securely into a high chair or other seat, using both waist and shoulder straps.

• How much your baby eats at this stage is less important than getting them used to the idea of new textures and tastes.

try
• Puréed cooked meat, poultry or white fish (watch out for bones)
• Cooked mashed pulses
• Cooked rice
• Cooked pasta (use baby pasta shapes)
• Cooked noodles (cut into short lengths)
• Well-cooked eggs (eggs should be cooked until the yolk and white are solid)
• Full-fat dairy products (e.g. natural yogurt; fromage frais; grated cheese)
• Cereals (e.g. porridge; wheat biscuit cereal)

Stage 3: around 7–8 months

If your baby seems ready, you can now move on to mashed, minced or finely chopped foods. Your baby may spit out the lumps at first but gradually they will learn to chew them. At this stage your baby should be having three meals a day.

- Never leave your baby alone while eating because of the risk of choking.
- Do not give your baby any food they could choke on. This includes popcorn, whole hot dogs and cocktail sausages, nuts and seeds, and large chunks of meat. Grapes (buy seedless ones) and cherry tomatoes should be sliced in half lengthwise.

Stage 4: 9–12 months

By the end of this stage, your baby will be able to eat a mixed diet, providing that everything is chopped. Try to give plenty of variety – eating a varied diet is the best way to ensure that your baby gets all the nutrients they need. Throughout the weaning process, milk will continue to be an important food in your baby's diet, but gradually the amount, variety and texture of foods eaten will increase. By around their first birthday, your baby will be able to eat much the same as the rest of the family, but will still be taking about 600 ml/1 pint of milk a day.

- It's important to let your baby join in with feeding – it can be a very messy business, so do be prepared. Wait until your baby has finished the meal before cleaning them up. Constantly wiping a baby's face can be frustrating for them and make mealtimes less enjoyable.
- Encourage your baby to use a spoon to feed themselves. Use a collecting bib to help cut down on the mess.
- Try not to rush mealtimes – it is a good idea to eat at the same time as your baby is having their meal.
- From the age of about 9 months, your baby's mealtimes can be adjusted to fit in with the normal family meals. Sharing family meals will allow your baby to enjoy social contact with the rest of the family and provides a good opportunity to learn social skills and table manners.

eating a balanced diet

What is a healthy balanced diet?

Every parent wants to do the best they can for their child and, when it comes to their health, one of the most important things you can do is to provide a healthy balanced diet. This will provide all the nutrients vital for growth and development as well as laying down the foundations for good health later in life. As well as helping children grow and stay healthy, the right diet will protect against diseases such as heart disease, diabetes and even some types of cancer later in life.

Although it's never too early to begin thinking about a healthy diet, babies and young children have small stomachs and high energy and nutrient requirements. This means that the healthy eating advice given to adults is not appropriate for babies and small children because high-fibre, low-fat diets can make it difficult for them to eat enough to meet their nutritional needs.

Making sure babies and young children eat a varied diet, with foods from each of the main food groups, is the best way to ensure they get all the nutrients they need for healthy growth and development.

Grains, cereals and potatoes

This group includes all types of bread, pasta, rice, noodles, couscous, potatoes and breakfast cereals.

- Foods containing gluten (including wheat, oats, barley and rye) should not be given until after the age of 6 months.

- From about the age of 9 months, your baby should eat three to four servings from this group each day.

Fruit and vegetables

This group includes fresh, frozen, canned fruit and vegetables and dried fruits. Fruit juice is also included in this group, but is best diluted and preferably served with a meal.

- From about the age of 9 months, your baby should eat three to four servings from this group each day.

- Vitamin C in fruit and vegetables will help your baby to absorb iron from other foods, so make sure you offer some fruit and vegetables at mealtimes.

Meat, fish and alternatives

This group includes meat, fish, eggs, tofu and pulses (peas, beans and lentils). Foods in this group provide protein, iron and zinc, as well as other important minerals and some vitamins.

• From about the age of 9 months, your baby should eat two servings from this group each day.

Milk and dairy foods

This group includes milk, cheese, yogurt and fromage frais. These foods are important sources of calcium, an essential mineral for growing bones and healthy teeth.

• Children under the age of 2 should be given full-fat milk and dairy products rather than low-fat or reduced-fat products. Growing babies and toddlers need lots of calories so low-fat milks are not suitable. Semi-skimmed milk can be introduced after the age of 2 years (provided your child has a good appetite and a varied diet) and skimmed milk after the age of 5 (again, if the child is eating well). Before you introduce either, it's best to discuss it with your health visitor.

• Cow's milk can be introduced after the age of 6 months, but experts recommend that breast or formula milk is preferable for the first year of life. A good compromise is to use cow's milk for cooking and adding to cereals, and formula or breast milk for drinking.

• After 6 months you can introduce follow-on milk. This has been specially designed to meet the increased nutritional needs of older babies and it contains more iron and vitamin D and less saturated fat than full-fat cow's milk.

• Until the age of 5 years, babies and children need approximately 600 ml/1 pint of milk a day. Continue with breast milk or infant formula or, after 6 months, use a follow-on milk.

Foods containing saturated fat and sugar

Foods in this group include crisps, biscuits and sweets and should only be eaten occasionally in very small amounts. Foods and drinks containing sugar, even the natural sugars present in fruit and fruit juices, should be consumed mainly at mealtimes to reduce the risk of tooth decay. Babies and young children need some fat in their diet but you should make sure it is healthy fat, like the type found in avocados, olive oil and oil-rich fish, rather than saturated fats found in foods like crisps, biscuits and cakes.

Foods to avoid

- You should never add **salt** to foods for babies. Even if the food tastes bland to you, it will be fine for your baby. Do not use **stock cubes** or **gravy granules** as they can be high in salt (see page 14 for vegetable stock recipe). Check the sodium/salt content on ready-prepared foods – babies under 12 months should consume less than 1 g of salt per day.

- Avoid canned foods that contain **added sugar** or **added salt**. Use canned sweetcorn or beans in water, and canned fruit in natural juice rather than syrup. Canned fish, such as tuna, should be packed in spring water or oil and not in brine.

- Don't add **sugar** or **sweeteners** to your baby's food. Adding sugar can encourage a sweet tooth and lead to tooth decay. Sweeteners, such as agave syrup, brown sugar, honey, evaporated cane juice or fructose, are no healthier than sugar. Babies should not be given **honey** until they are at least 12 months old because it can contain a type of bacteria that can cause serious illness.

- Foods containing **gluten** (including bread, pasta and some breakfast cereals) should not be introduced until after the age of 6 months.

- Children under 5 should not be given **whole nuts** as they may cause choking. Nut butters and crushed or ground nuts are okay.

- **Unpasteurized milk and cheeses** are not suitable for the under 1s.

- **Low-fat foods** are not suitable for babies and children under the age of 2 because fat is an important source of calories and some vitamins.

- **Raw and lightly cooked eggs** should be avoided. Eggs can be given to babies over 6 months, but make sure they are thoroughly cooked until both the white and yolk are solid.

- Babies should not be given **shark, swordfish or marlin**. This is because the relatively high levels of mercury in these fish can affect a baby's growing nervous system.

- **Raw meat, fish and shellfish** should not be given to children under the age of 5 years because of an increased risk of food poisoning.

- **Liver** should be limited to one small serving a week because of high levels of vitamin A.

Healthy eating tips

- It's important to start good eating habits early in life as it can be hard to change bad habits once they're established.
- Vitamin drops with vitamins A and D are recommended for all children between the ages of 1 to 5 years. Breast-fed babies and babies drinking less than 500 ml/18 fl oz of infant formula milk per day should be given vitamin drops from 6 months, or earlier if advised by your health visitor or doctor.
- Up to the age of 12 months, babies are much more receptive to new tastes and new foods, so it's important to use the opportunity to introduce a wide variety of foods with different tastes and textures.
- Well-diluted fruit juice, rather than water, can be offered with vegetarian meals as the vitamin C will increase the absorption of iron from vegetables and cereal foods.
- Drinks from bottles should be cut out around 12 months and all drinks should be offered from cups or beakers. About 100–125 ml/3½–4 fl oz is the average-sized drink for a baby over 12 months.
- Offer 6–8 drinks (water, diluted fruit juice or milk) a day – one drink with each meal and one between meals or with snacks.

Food allergies and intolerances

If either parent or sibling has asthma, eczema, a food allergy or intolerance, your baby has a greater risk of also suffering from the same condition. If you suspect your baby may be more likely to have an allergy, you should make sure that the first foods you introduce are low-allergenic foods, such as rice, potatoes, green vegetables, apples, pears, bananas and stone fruit. Once weaning is well established, you can then start to introduce foods that are more likely to cause problems. These include:

- Dairy products (e.g. cow's milk; yogurt; fromage frais; cheese)
- Wheat and gluten
- Eggs
- Fish and shellfish
- Nuts
- Sesame seeds
- Soy
- Celery
- Foods containing sulphite preservatives (e.g. jellies, some drinks and dried apricots)
- Citrus fruits
- Tomatoes
- Strawberries

These foods should be introduced one at a time and you should continue with each new food for two or three consecutive days before you introduce another so that you can monitor any reaction. It is important that food allergies and intolerances are properly diagnosed – if you are concerned that your child is developing a food allergy or intolerance, consult a qualified medical professional.

vegetable stock

Prepare:
10 minutes

Cook:
25–30 minutes

Makes:
1 litre/1¾ pints

ingredients

1 garlic clove
1 onion
1 carrot
1 celery stick
4 black peppercorns
handful of fresh flat-leaf parsley sprigs
1 litre/1¾ pints water

Peel the garlic and onion and chop roughly. Peel and trim the carrot and cut into large chunks. Trim the celery and cut into chunky pieces.

Place the prepared vegetables in a saucepan with the peppercorns, parsley and water.

Cover and bring to the boil, then reduce the heat and simmer for 25–30 minutes. Remove from the heat and leave to cool.

Strain through a sieve, discarding the cooked vegetables. Use immediately or store for up to 48 hours in the refrigerator or up to 8 weeks in the freezer.

equipment

Preparing home-made baby food doesn't have to take a great deal of time or require much equipment but, if you don't already own one, it is worth investing in a **blender** or **food processor**. Alternatively, you could try a **hand-held blender** for puréeing foods directly in the saucepan. In the first stage of weaning you may also wish to press the purée through a **mouli** or **sieve** to remove any fibres or pips and, in the case of peas and beans, to separate out the indigestible skins.

When you first start weaning, your baby probably will only eat a couple of teaspoonfuls of food at each meal but it's a good idea to make a batch of purée and freeze small amounts in **ice-cube trays** so you can take out just a couple of cubes at a time when you need them. If you're making up several batches, you can remove the cubes from the trays once frozen and transfer them to **re-sealable freezer bags** to store them. As your baby gets older and starts to eat more, you can use small **freezerproof containers** with tightly fitting lids to store food. Make sure you mark the containers with the contents and the date it was frozen. Most home-made baby foods can be kept in the refrigerator for up to 48 hours or in the freezer for up to 8 weeks.

food safety

Good food hygiene is important for everyone but when you are preparing and cooking food for babies it is obviously more important than ever.

- Before you start preparing food, always wash your hands thoroughly with hot water and an antibacterial handwash, then dry them with a clean towel.
- Make sure all your equipment is as clean as possible. If you have decided to wean your baby before they are 6 months old, all equipment should be sterilized. Once your baby is 6 months old, there is no need to sterilize their bowls and cutlery. If you have a dishwasher, all equipment should be placed on the top shelf and washed using the highest temperature setting (but check it is dishwasher-proof first). If you are hand-washing, use hot, soapy water.
- Always wash your hands in between touching raw and cooked foods. Use separate knives, chopping boards and utensils for preparing raw and cooked foods or wash them thoroughly in hot, soapy water.
- Store raw and cooked foods on separate shelves in the refrigerator, making sure that any raw foods cannot drip on to cooked foods.
- If you are preparing food to be frozen, freeze it as soon as possible after cooking but never put hot food straight into the refrigerator or freezer. If you are cooking a large quantity of food to freeze, it will cool much quicker if it is divided into smaller portions, or transferred into a container with a large surface area. During warm weather, place the container into a bowl of iced water. Food should be cooled and refrigerated within 1 hour of being cooked.
- Never refreeze food that has been frozen previously, unless it has been cooked in between (e.g. if a frozen raw meat, such as beef mince, is defrosted and cooked to make something like a Bolognese sauce, the cooked dish can be refrozen).
- If you are using a jar or bottle of baby food, use a clean spoon to transfer the amount you need to a small bowl. Throw away any food that your baby doesn't eat – do not return it to the container.
- Heat food thoroughly and allow it to cool before feeding it to your baby. Heat home-made food in a microwave or in a pan on the hob until it is piping hot. Stir the food well and test the temperature before offering it to your baby (this is especially important if you used a microwave to heat it). If you are using jars of baby food, stand them in a pan of hot water to heat them up. Never reheat food more than once and throw away any leftovers.

chapter 1
fruit

My baby's photo here

First fruit baby tasted:

....

....

....

....

Baby's favourite fruit/recipe:

....

....

....

....

Memorable moments:

....

....

....

....

go bananas

Bananas are rich in potassium and slow-release carbohydrates. They also have the added advantage of coming in their own packaging, making them a perfectly portable food for babies (and parents) on the go!

 Prepare:
5 minutes

 Cook:
0 minutes

 Servings:
1

ingredients

½ small ripe banana
dash of full-fat
milk (optional)

Peel the banana and mash with a fork until smooth. If desired, mix the banana with a little milk for a runnier consistency.

Serve immediately. Do not refrigerate or freeze.

my notes:

....

....

....

melon purée

Any variety of melon can be given to babies, providing it's sweet and juicy. Orange-fleshed melons, such as charentais and canteloupe, are a particularly good source of beta-carotene and are also high in vitamin C.

Prepare:
5 minutes

Cook:
0 minutes

Servings:
1

ingredients

small wedge of melon

Scoop out the seeds from the melon and remove the skin. Cut the flesh into chunks and blend until smooth.

Serve immediately or store in the refrigerator until required but use on day of making. Do not freeze.

tip
It may be necessary to steam the fruit if it's not entirely ripe.

my notes:

....

....

....

mango tango

Mangoes are rich in vitamin C and contain a significant amount of the antioxidant vitamin E, which can boost the body's immune system and maintain healthy skin. They are a good introduction to tropical fruit too.

Prepare:
5 minutes

Cook:
0 minutes

Servings:
2–3

ingredients

1 small ripe mango

Peel, stone and slice the mango. Mash with a fork until smooth and press through a sieve or mouli to remove the fibres.

Serve immediately or store for up to 48 hours in the refrigerator or up to 8 weeks in the freezer.

tip
If you buy an unripe mango, put it in a paper bag in a dark place and it will ripen within a few days.

my notes:

....

....

....

purely pear

It has been found that eating pears is less likely to produce an allergic response than eating many other fruits, making them a great weaning food. Very ripe pears do not need to be cooked.

Prepare:
5 minutes

Cook:
5–8 minutes

Servings:
2–3

ingredients

1 small ripe pear
2 tbsp water

Peel, core and dice the pear. Put the pear into a saucepan with the water. Bring to the boil and cook for 5–8 minutes, until the fruit is tender.

Drain the pear, reserving the cooking water, and blend until smooth. If necessary, thin with a little of the reserved cooking water.

Serve lukewarm or store for up to 48 hours in the refrigerator or up to 8 weeks in the freezer.

my notes:

....

....

....

creamy avocado

The avocado is a rich source of monosaturated fats for heart health and is packed with important nutrients. If your baby is not keen on avocado on its own, try mixing it with banana.

 Prepare:
5 minutes

 Cook:
0 minutes

 Servings:
1

ingredients

½ small ripe avocado

dash of full-fat milk (optional)

Remove the stone from the avocado and scoop out the flesh with a spoon. Mash with a fork until smooth. If desired, mix the avocado with a little milk for a runnier consistency.

Serve immediately. Do not refrigerate or freeze.

tip
You will need to prepare this purée just before serving because avocado flesh discolours very quickly after it has been cut.

my notes:

....

....

....

my notes:

....

....

....

amazing apricot & prune purée

Dried fruits, such as apricots and prunes, have a natural sweetness that babies love. Their high fibre content means that they can help with constipation as they are a natural laxative.

 Prepare:
5 minutes + soaking

 Cook:
10 minutes

 Servings:
2–3

ingredients

6 dried apricots,
soaked overnight

2–3 pitted prunes,
soaked overnight

Drain the apricots and prunes, discarding the soaking water. Put them in a saucepan with enough boiling water to cover. Bring to the boil, then reduce the heat and simmer for 10 minutes, or until very tender.

Drain the apricots and prunes, reserving the cooking water. If wished, press the mixture through a sieve or mouli to remove any skins. If necessary, thin with a little of the reserved cooking water.

Serve lukewarm or store for up to 48 hours in the refrigerator or up to 8 weeks in the freezer.

tip
You may prefer to choose unsulphured dried apricots because the sulphite preservatives used to retain the bright orange colour of the fruit can trigger asthma or allergies in susceptible babies.

apple & pear combo

Apples and pears are closely related and blend well together. In common with bananas and stone fruit, they are considered to be low-allergenic, so are particularly suitable as first fruits for young children.

 Prepare:
5 minutes

 Cook:
7–10 minutes

 Servings:
4–6

ingredients

1 eating apple
1 ripe pear
3 tbsp water

Peel, core and dice the apple and pear. Put all the ingredients into a saucepan and bring to the boil. Reduce the heat, cover and simmer for about 7–10 minutes, until very soft. Check regularly to make sure that the fruit has not caught on the bottom of the saucepan. Leave to cool a little.

Drain the fruit, reserving the cooking water, and blend until smooth. If necessary, thin with a little of the reserved cooking water.

Serve lukewarm or store for up to 48 hours in the refrigerator or up to 8 weeks in the freezer.

tip
It is best to choose a sweet eating apple for this recipe rather than a cooking apple, which will be too tart and acidic for delicate tummies.

my notes:

....

....

....

31

orchard fruit purée

Apples, pears and peaches combine perfectly together in this popular and easy-to-digest baby purée. If the mixture is a little on the runny side, try mixing it with some baby rice.

 Prepare:
5–10 minutes

 Cook:
7–10 minutes

 Servings:
4–6

ingredients

1 small eating apple
1 small ripe pear
3 tbsp water
1 small ripe peach

Peel, core and dice the apple and pear. Put into a saucepan with the water and bring to the boil. Reduce the heat, cover and simmer for about 7–10 minutes, until very soft. Check regularly to make sure that the fruit has not caught on the bottom of the saucepan. Leave to cool a little.

Meanwhile, score a cross on the base of the peach and drop into a bowl of boiling water. Leave to stand for 1–2 minutes, then drain. Peel off the skin from the peach and chop the flesh, removing and discarding the stone.

Drain the apple and pear, reserving the cooking water, and blend with the peach until smooth. If necessary, thin with a little of the reserved cooking water.

Serve lukewarm or store for up to 48 hours in the refrigerator or up to 8 weeks in the freezer.

my notes:

....

....

....

my notes:

....

....

....

peach melba purée

Raspberries provide good amounts of vitamin C, which is important for a healthy immune system. Serving foods rich in vitamin C with cereals, such as baby rice, will help your baby to absorb iron.

 Prepare:
5 minutes

 Cook:
12–15 minutes

 Servings:
4

ingredients

2 ripe peaches
4 tbsp water
100 g/3½ oz raspberries

Score a cross on the bases of the peaches and drop into a bowl of boiling water. Leave to stand for 1–2 minutes, then drain. Peel off the skins from the peaches and chop the flesh, removing and discarding the stones. Place the chopped peaches in a small saucepan with the water.

Cover and gently cook for 8–10 minutes. Check regularly to make sure the fruit has not caught on the bottom of the saucepan.

Add the raspberries and continue cooking for a further 4–5 minutes, until the fruit is soft.

Blend until smooth. If wished, press the mixture through a sieve or mouli to remove the raspberry pips.

Serve lukewarm or store for up to 48 hours in the refrigerator or up to 8 weeks in the freezer.

gooey banana & blueberry purée

Bananas contain a type of dietary fibre called
fructooligosaccharides, which encourages the
growth of friendly bacteria in the digestive
system. They are also incredibly yummy!

 Prepare:
5 minutes

 Cook:
5 minutes

 Servings:
1

ingredients

25 g/1 oz blueberries
1 tbsp water
½ ripe banana

Put the blueberries in a small saucepan
with the water. Place over a medium heat
and simmer gently for 5 minutes, stirring
occasionally, until the berries have started
to burst.

Blend until smooth. If wished, press the mixture
through a sieve or mouli to remove the
blueberry skins. Leave to cool a little.

Peel the banana and mash with a fork until
smooth, then combine with the puréed
blueberries.

Serve immediately. Do not refrigerate or freeze.

my notes:

36

autumn harvest heaven

Orange and red fruits and vegetables, such as pumpkin, squash, apricots and red peppers, are rich in carotenoids. These carotenoids are important for a healthy immune system and skin.

 Prepare:
10 minutes

 Cook:
15–20 minutes

 Servings:
2–3

ingredients

1 eating apple
125 g/4½ oz butternut squash
150 ml/5 fl oz full-fat milk
pinch of ground cinnamon (optional)

Peel, core and dice the apple. Peel, deseed and finely dice the butternut squash.

Place the apple, butternut squash and milk in a small pan over a medium heat. Cover and simmer for 15–20 minutes, until everything is soft.

Blend until smooth, then stir in the cinnamon, if using.

Serve lukewarm or store for up to 48 hours in the refrigerator or up to 8 weeks in the freezer.

tip
Some babies can be sensitive to cinnamon so, if you aren't sure, leave it out.

my notes:

squashed tomatoes & sweetcorn

Canned and frozen fruit and vegetables are fine for babies. However, make sure you choose fruit that is canned in fruit juice or water, rather than syrup, and vegetables that are canned without added salt or sugar.

 Prepare:
5 minutes

 Cook:
20 minutes

 Servings:
4

ingredients

10 g/¼ oz unsalted butter or polyunsaturated margarine

½ bunch of spring onions, trimmed and chopped

400 g/14 oz canned chopped tomatoes

150 g/5½ oz sweetcorn kernels, canned in water and drained, or frozen

1 tbsp finely chopped fresh basil

Melt the butter in a saucepan over a medium heat and sauté the spring onions for 3–4 minutes, until starting to soften.

Add the tomatoes and sweetcorn, cover and simmer for 15 minutes, adding the basil in the last few minutes. Blend until smooth. If wished, press the mixture through a sieve or mouli to remove the sweetcorn skins.

Serve lukewarm or store for up to 48 hours in the refrigerator or up to 8 weeks in the freezer.

my notes:

....

....

....

amazing apple & cauliflower

Apples and cauliflower are a tasty combination. They are both good sources of gentle fibres, which help to keep your baby's digestive system healthy and prevent constipation.

 Prepare:
10 minutes

 Cook:
12–15 minutes

 Servings:
3–4

ingredients

1 eating apple
115 g/4 oz cauliflower
125 ml/4 fl oz full-fat milk

Peel, core and dice the apple. Trim the cauliflower, removing and discarding the thick stalk. Cut the cauliflower first into small florets, then slice these thinly.

Place the apple and cauliflower in a small saucepan over a medium heat. Add the milk, cover and simmer for 12–15 minutes, until soft. Blend until smooth.

Serve lukewarm or store for up to 48 hours in the refrigerator or up to 8 weeks in the freezer.

my notes:

....

....

....

pear baby rice delight

Baby rice is ideal when starting to wean your baby because it has a low allergic reaction rate and a simple flavour. Don't be tempted to add salt or sugar, even if it tastes bland to you.

 Prepare:
5–10 minutes

 Cook:
5–10 minutes

 Servings:
1

ingredients

1 ripe pear
3 tbsp water
10 g/¼ oz baby rice

Peel, core and dice the pear and place in a small saucepan with the water. Cook gently for 5–10 minutes, until the fruit is completely soft. Leave to cool a little.

Mash the pear, then stir in the baby rice until the mixture is smooth. Depending on the ripeness of the pear, there should be enough cooking water to rehydrate the rice. If not, add a little more water.

Serve immediately. Do not refrigerate or freeze.

tip
To prepare plain baby rice, place 1 tablespoon of baby rice in a clean bowl. Add 3 tablespoons of your baby's usual milk, either cold or warmed. Mix well until you have a smooth consistency. Use within 30 minutes.

my notes:
....
....
....

45

my notes:

....

....

....

sweet apricot & banana baby rice

Apricots are rich in beta-carotene, which the body can convert into vitamin A. Vitamin A has a number of important functions, such as the development of healthy eyes and skin.

 Prepare: 5 minutes

 Cook: 10–12 minutes

 Servings: 1

ingredients

2 small fresh apricots
2 tbsp water
10 g/¼ oz baby rice
½ small ripe banana

Score a cross on the bases of the apricots and drop into a bowl of boiling water. Leave to stand for 1–2 minutes, then drain. Peel off the skins from the apricots and chop the flesh, removing and discarding the stones. Place the chopped apricots in a small saucepan with the water.

Cover and simmer gently for 9–10 minutes, until very soft. Check regularly to make sure that the fruit has not caught on the bottom of the saucepan. Leave to cool a little.

Blend until smooth. Stir the baby rice into the apricot purée.

Peel the banana and mash with a fork until smooth, then combine with the apricot and rice mixture.

Serve immediately. Do not refrigerate or freeze.

purple porridge

Oats are a highly nutritious choice at breakfast time
(or at any time of the day!) as they release their
energy slowly, making little tummies feel full for
longer. Berries are rich in antioxidants.

 Prepare:
5 minutes

 Cook:
5 minutes

 Servings:
1

ingredients

50 g/1¾ oz mixed
berries, such as
raspberries, strawberries,
blackberries and
blueberries

15 g/½ oz rolled oats

50 ml/2 fl oz full-fat milk

Hull the strawberries, if using, and check
over the remaining berries to make sure all
the stalks have been removed. Blend all the
berries until smooth. If wished, press the mixture
through a sieve or mouli to remove any pips or
skins. For older babies, you can reserve some
of the berries and chop into small chunks to
add texture.

Put the oats and milk into a small saucepan
and bring to the boil. Reduce the heat and
simmer gently, stirring occasionally, for
5 minutes, or until thickened. Leave to cool
a little.

Pour the porridge into a serving bowl and stir in
the fruit purée. Scatter over the chopped fruit,
if using.

Serve lukewarm or store for up to 48 hours in
the refrigerator. Do not freeze.

my notes:

....

....

....

dried apricot porridge

You may prefer to use unsulphured dried apricots in this recipe as sulphur dioxide can trigger asthma or allergies in susceptible babies. Try using dates for a delicious alternative.

 Prepare:
5 minutes + soaking

 Cook:
10 minutes

 Servings:
2

ingredients

4 dried apricots, soaked overnight and drained

30 g/1 oz rolled oats

100 ml/3½ fl oz full-fat milk

Put the apricots in a saucepan with enough boiling water to cover. Bring to the boil, then reduce the heat and simmer for 10 minutes, or until very tender.

Meanwhile, put the oats and milk into a small saucepan and bring to the boil. Reduce the heat and simmer gently, stirring occasionally, for 5 minutes, or until thickened. Leave to cool a little.

Drain the apricots, reserving the cooking water. If wished, press the apricots through a sieve or mouli to remove any skins. If necessary, thin with a little of the reserved cooking water. Pour the porridge into a serving bowl and stir in the apricot purée.

Serve lukewarm or store for up to 48 hours in the refrigerator. Do not freeze.

my notes:

....

....

....

mango swirl yogurt

Yogurt is an excellent source of calcium, but many shop-bought yogurts contain added sugar so are best avoided. Mixing natural yogurt with fruit purée takes away its slight bitter aftertaste and makes it more palatable for babies.

 Prepare:
5 minutes

 Cook:
0 minutes

 Servings:
2

ingredients

½ small ripe mango
4–6 tbsp full-fat
natural yogurt
1 tsp wheatgerm
(optional)

Peel, stone and slice the mango. Mash with a fork until smooth. If wished, press through a sieve or mouli to remove the fibres.

Swirl the mango purée into the yogurt and sprinkle with the wheatgerm, if using.

Serve immediately or store for up to 48 hours in the refrigerator. Do not freeze.

my notes:

....

....

....

yum yum apple & plum yogurt

Some babies dislike the texture of plums, so mixing them with apple and yogurt is a good idea to make them more baby friendly. Fully ripe plums contain more antioxidants than semi-ripe ones.

 Prepare: 5 minutes

 Cook: 5 minutes

 Servings: 2

ingredients

1 small eating apple
2 ripe plums
2 tbsp water
4–6 tbsp full-fat natural yogurt

Peel, core and dice the apple. Halve and stone the plums. Put the apple and plums into a small saucepan with the water and bring to the boil. Reduce the heat, cover and simmer for about 5 minutes, until tender.

Blend until smooth. If wished, press the mixture through a sieve or mouli to remove the plum skins.

Swirl the apple and plum purée into the yogurt.

Serve immediately or store for up to 48 hours in the refrigerator. Do not freeze.

my notes:

....

....

....

dreamy banana yogurt

Bananas, when they are well ripened, are easy for your baby to digest and can be mashed into a smooth paste. This dessert is the perfect way to introduce yogurt into your child's diet.

 Prepare:
5 minutes

 Cook:
0 minutes

 Servings:
1

ingredients

½ small ripe banana

a few drops of
vanilla extract

2–3 tbsp full-fat
Greek-style yogurt

Peel the banana and mash with a fork until smooth.

Stir the vanilla extract into the banana purée, then layer with the yogurt in a small serving bowl.

Serve immediately. Do not refrigerate or freeze.

my notes:

56

chapter 2
vegetables

My baby's photo here

First vegetable baby tasted:

....

....

....

....

Baby's favourite vegetable/recipe:

....

....

....

....

Memorable moments:

....

....

....

....

see-in-the-dark purée

Root vegetables, such as carrots and sweet potatoes, are ideal as first weaning foods because they are naturally sweet. Carrots contain a good range of vitamins and minerals and help to keep the eyes healthy.

 Prepare: 5 minutes

 Cook: 10–15 minutes

 Servings: 1–2

ingredients

1 carrot, about 100 g/3½ oz

dash of full-fat milk (optional)

Peel the carrot and cut into 3-mm/⅛-inch dice. Steam or cook in enough unsalted boiling water just to cover for about 10–15 minutes, or until soft.

Drain the carrot, reserving the cooking water, and blend until smooth. If necessary, thin with a little of the reserved cooking water or some milk, if using.

Serve lukewarm or store for up to 48 hours in the refrigerator or up to 8 weeks in the freezer.

my notes:

summer squash purée

Courgette can be a difficult vegetable to introduce to your child, so it is best not to leave it until too long into the weaning process before you offer it. It can be combined with potato to make it more palatable.

Prepare:
5 minutes

Cook:
4–5 minutes

Servings:
2

ingredients

1 courgette

Trim and slice the courgette – there is no need to peel it.

Steam or cook the courgette in enough unsalted boiling water just to cover for about 4–5 minutes, until tender. Leave to cool a little. Blend or mash with a fork until smooth.

Serve lukewarm or store for up to 48 hours in the refrigerator or up to 8 weeks in the freezer.

my notes:
....
....
....

winter warmer wonder

Sweet potatoes contain good amounts of the antioxidant vitamins C and E, as well as group B vitamins, beta-carotene, manganese and potassium. They have a sweet taste your baby will love.

 Prepare:
10 minutes

 Cook:
12–15 minutes

 Servings:
4–5

ingredients

225 g/8 oz sweet potato
200 g/7 oz turnip
175 ml/6 fl oz full-fat milk

Peel the sweet potato and turnip and cut into small cubes.

Place the vegetables and milk in a small saucepan over a medium heat. Cover and simmer for 12–15 minutes, until the vegetables are soft. Blend until smooth.

Serve lukewarm or store for up to 48 hours in the refrigerator or up to 8 weeks in the freezer.

my notes:

sunny sweetcorn
& pumpkin purée

Sweetcorn is a good source of folate, important for the manufacture of red blood cells. The skins can be difficult to digest so for younger babies it is important to pass the purée through a sieve or mouli to remove them.

 Prepare:
10 minutes

 Cook:
15–20 minutes

 Servings:
4–5

ingredients

300 g/10½ oz pumpkin or butternut squash

150 g/5½ oz sweetcorn kernels, canned in water and drained, or frozen

200 ml/7 fl oz full-fat milk

Peel the pumpkin and scoop out the seeds. Cut the flesh into small cubes and place in a saucepan.

Add the sweetcorn and milk to the pan and bring to simmering point. Cover and continue cooking gently for 15–20 minutes, until tender. Blend until smooth. If wished, press the mixture through a sieve or mouli to remove the sweetcorn skins.

Serve lukewarm or store for up to 48 hours in the refrigerator or up to 8 weeks in the freezer.

my notes:

green & white purée

Broccoli contains vitamins K (good for blood and bones),
B and C and is in the league of 'super foods'. If your
baby isn't keen on the taste, offer with a sweet-tasting
vegetable, such as sweet potato.

 Prepare:
5 minutes

 Cook:
7–10 minutes

 Servings:
2–3

ingredients

3 small broccoli florets
3 small cauliflower florets
dash of full-fat
milk (optional)

Remove and discard any hard stalks from
the broccoli and cauliflower, then roughly
chop the florets. Steam or cook in enough
unsalted boiling water just to cover for about
7–10 minutes, until tender. Leave to cool
a little.

Drain the broccoli and cauliflower, reserving
the cooking water, and blend until smooth.
If necessary, thin with a little of the reserved
cooking water or some milk, if using.

Serve lukewarm or store for up to 48 hours in
the refrigerator or up to 8 weeks in the freezer.

my notes:

squash & spinach smash

Orange-fleshed butternut squash is rich in carotenes and its sweet taste is very appealing to babies. Spinach doesn't contain as much iron as was once thought, nevertheless, it has many health benefits.

 Prepare:
5 minutes

 Cook:
20 minutes

 Servings:
2

ingredients

small wedge of
butternut squash
(about 100 g/3½ oz)

25 g/1 oz fresh spinach
leaves

dash of full-fat
milk (optional)

Peel the butternut squash and scoop out the seeds. Cut the flesh into small cubes. Remove any tough stalks from the spinach.

Steam or cook the squash in enough unsalted boiling water just to cover for about 15 minutes. Add the spinach and cook for a further 5 minutes.

Drain the squash and spinach, reserving the cooking water, and blend until smooth. If necessary, thin with a little of the reserved cooking water or some milk, if using.

Serve lukewarm or store for up to 48 hours in the refrigerator or up to 8 weeks in the freezer.

my notes:

....

....

....

super sweet potato & pea purée

Peas are a good source of protein, group B vitamins, vitamin C and dietary fibre. In addition, the vitamin C from the peas will make it easy for your baby to absorb the iron in the sweet potatoes.

 Prepare:
5 minutes

 Cook:
12–15 minutes

 Servings:
2–3

ingredients

175 g/6 oz sweet potato
100 ml/3½ fl oz vegetable stock (see page 14) or full-fat milk
150 g/5½ oz frozen peas

Peel the sweet potato and cut into small cubes.

Place the sweet potato and stock in a small saucepan over a medium heat. Cover and simmer for 10–12 minutes. Add the peas and continue cooking for a further 2–3 minutes, until soft.

Blend until smooth. If wished, press the mixture through a sieve or mouli to remove the pea skins.

Serve lukewarm or store for up to 48 hours in the refrigerator or up to 8 weeks in the freezer.

my notes:

....

....

....

spring green goodness

Frozen vegetables can be just as nutritious as fresh ones because they are frozen within hours of being picked. If you wish to use fresh peas for this recipe, add them to the pan along with the beans and courgette.

 Prepare:
5 minutes

 Cook:
10 minutes

 Servings:
2

ingredients

25 g/1 oz young
green beans
25 g/1 oz courgette
25 g/1 oz frozen peas

Trim and cut the beans into 2.5-cm/1-inch lengths. Trim and roughly chop the courgette – there is no need to peel it.

Steam or cook the beans and courgette in enough unsalted boiling water just to cover for about 6 minutes. Add the peas and cook for a further 4 minutes.

Drain the vegetables, reserving the cooking water, and blend until smooth. If necessary, thin with a little of the reserved cooking water. If wished, press the mixture through a sieve or mouli to remove any stringy bits from the beans and the pea skins.

Serve lukewarm or store for up to 48 hours in the refrigerator or up to 8 weeks in the freezer.

my notes:

power pea & carrot purée

The antioxidant beta-carotene gives carrots their characteristic orange colour. In the body, beta-carotene can also be converted into vitamin A, which is important for healthy skin and eyes.

 Prepare:
5 minutes

 Cook:
15–20 minutes

 Servings:
3–4

ingredients

200 g/7 oz carrots
200 ml/7 fl oz vegetable stock (see page 14) or full-fat milk
200 g/7 oz frozen peas

Peel and finely chop the carrots. Place the carrots and stock in a small saucepan over a medium heat. Cover and simmer for 12–15 minutes.

Add the peas and cook for a further 2–3 minutes, until everything is soft. Blend until smooth. If wished, press the mixture through a sieve or mouli to remove the pea skins.

Serve lukewarm or store for up to 48 hours in the refrigerator or up to 8 weeks in the freezer.

my notes:
....
....
....

cauliflower, leek & potato combo

Leeks boast many of the health benefits of onions, but with a milder taste. Make sure that you wash them thoroughly before using – they may contain soil between the tight leaves.

 Prepare: 5 minutes

 Cook: 15–20 minutes

 Servings: 4–6

ingredients

1 potato
3 small cauliflower florets
½ small leek
dash of full-fat milk (optional)

Peel and dice the potato. Remove and discard any hard stalks from the cauliflower. Trim the leek and discard the tough outer layer, then slice thinly.

Steam or cook the vegetables in enough unsalted boiling water just to cover for about 15–20 minutes, until tender.

Drain the vegetables, reserving the cooking water, and blend until smooth. If necessary, thin with a little of the reserved cooking water or some milk, if using.

Serve lukewarm or store for up to 48 hours in the refrigerator or up to 8 weeks in the freezer.

my notes:

....

....

....

79

not-just-for-breakfast porridge

This wholesome purée proves that oats can be eaten at any time of the day! Oats are nutritional super heroes – they help to stabilize blood sugar, they are rich in soluble fibre and they provide a source of healthy fats.

 Prepare:
5 minutes

 Cook:
10–15 minutes

 Servings:
4–6

ingredients

1 small leek
1 tomato
30 g/1 oz rolled oats
50 ml/2 fl oz water
50 ml/2 fl oz full-fat milk, plus extra if needed
2 tbsp frozen sweetcorn
small knob of unsalted butter or polyunsaturated margarine

Trim the leek and discard the tough outer layer, then finely chop. Score a cross on the base of the tomato and drop into a bowl of boiling water. Leave to stand for 1–2 minutes, then drain. Peel off the skin from the tomato, deseed and finely chop the flesh.

Put the oats, water and milk into a small saucepan and bring to the boil. Reduce the heat and simmer, stirring occasionally, for 5 minutes, or until thickened.

Meanwhile, steam or cook the leek in enough unsalted boiling water just to cover for about 10–15 minutes, until tender. Drain the leek and return to the pan with the cooked oats, sweetcorn, tomato and butter. Stir until thoroughly combined and heated through. Blend until smooth, thinning with a little extra milk, if necessary. If wished, press the mixture through a sieve or mouli to remove the sweetcorn skins.

Serve lukewarm or store for up to 48 hours in the refrigerator or up to 8 weeks in the freezer.

my notes:

....

....

....

popeye's purée

Although spinach doesn't contain as much iron as once thought, it is still a good source of several other nutrients. These include group B vitamins and vitamin K, which is important for healthy blood and bones.

 Prepare:
5 minutes

 Cook:
12–15 minutes

 Servings:
5–6

ingredients

200 g/7 oz potatoes
150 g/5½ oz eating apple
55 g/2 oz fresh
spinach leaves
200 ml/7 fl oz full-fat milk

Peel and cube the potatoes. Peel, core and dice the apple. Remove any tough stalks from the spinach.

Place the potatoes, apple and milk in a saucepan over a medium heat. Cover and gently simmer for 10–12 minutes, until the potatoes are almost tender.

Add the spinach, re-cover and simmer for a further 2–3 minutes, until it has wilted and the potatoes are tender. Blend until smooth.

Serve lukewarm or store for up to 48 hours in the refrigerator or up to 8 weeks in the freezer.

my notes:

....

....

....

my notes:

....

....

....

courgette & avocado blend

Avocado pears are an excellent weaning food because they contain large amounts of predominantly healthy fats. They are also a good source of vitamin E and vitamin B6.

 Prepare: 5 minutes

 Cook: 8–10 minutes

 Servings: 1

ingredients

50 g/1 ¾ oz courgette
½ ripe avocado

Trim and roughly chop the courgette – there is no need to peel it.

Steam or cook the courgette in enough unsalted boiling water just to cover for 8–10 minutes. Drain, reserving the cooking water, and leave to cool a little.

Remove the stone from the avocado and scoop out the flesh with a spoon. Chop the flesh, then add to the courgette and blend until smooth. If necessary, thin with a little of the reserved cooking water.

Serve immediately. Do not refrigerate or freeze.

my notes:

....

....

....

love your lentils

Red lentils are a good source of protein and dietary fibre, which is important for maintaining a healthy digestive system. They also provide good amounts of iron and potassium.

 Prepare:
10 minutes

 Cook:
20–25 minutes

 Servings:
4–5

ingredients

100 g/3½ oz red lentils
200 g/7 oz carrots
400 ml/14 fl oz vegetable stock (see page 14) or water
juice and finely grated rind of 1 orange

Place the lentils in a sieve and wash under cold running water. Peel and chop the carrots.

Place the lentils and carrots in a small saucepan and pour over the stock. Cover, bring to the boil and allow to boil rapidly for 10 minutes. Reduce the heat and simmer for a further 10–15 minutes, until everything is soft.

Stir in the orange juice and rind and blend until smooth.

Serve lukewarm or store for up to 48 hours in the refrigerator or up to 8 weeks in the freezer.

my notes:

....
....
....

super-tasty cauliflower cheese

Milk and cheese are good sources of calcium, which is needed for healthy bones and teeth. Reduced-fat dairy products are not suitable for babies and young children as they need the fat to meet their energy needs.

 Prepare:
5 minutes

 Cook:
12–15 minutes

 Servings:
2–3

ingredients

300 g/10½ oz cauliflower

200 ml/7 fl oz full-fat milk

70 g/2½ oz mature Cheddar cheese

Trim the cauliflower, discarding the thick stalk. Cut into small florets, then slice thinly. Put into a small saucepan and pour over the milk. Place over a medium heat, cover and cook for 12–15 minutes, until soft.

Grate the cheese. When the cauliflower is cooked, stir in the cheese and blend until smooth.

Serve lukewarm or store for up to 48 hours in the refrigerator or up to 8 weeks in the freezer.

my notes:

....

....

....

five-veggie sauce
with pasta

This tasty sauce is the perfect accompaniment to pasta. Use tiny pasta shapes designed for babies, such as pasta stars, until your baby is ready for something a little chunkier.

 Prepare:
10 minutes

 Cook:
30 minutes

 Servings:
4–6

ingredients

1 tbsp vegetable oil

1 small onion, finely chopped

1 small carrot, peeled and finely chopped

½ red pepper, deseeded and finely chopped

1 small courgette, trimmed and finely chopped

100 ml/3½ fl oz vegetable stock (see page 14) or water

200 ml/7 fl oz passata

2–3 fresh basil leaves, chopped

85 g/3 oz baby pasta shapes

Heat the oil in a saucepan over a medium heat and cook the onion and carrot for 5 minutes. Add the red pepper and courgette and cook for 1–2 minutes. Add the stock, cover and simmer for 15 minutes. Add the passata and basil and cook until the sauce has reduced and thickened. Blend the sauce to the desired consistency.

Meanwhile, cook the pasta according to the packet instructions until it is tender. Drain and return to the pan, then stir in the sauce.

Serve lukewarm or store for up to 48 hours in the refrigerator or up to 8 weeks in the freezer.

my notes:

....

....

....

91

butternut pasta

Butternut squash is easily digested and has a naturally sweet taste that tends to be very popular with babies. You could also make this recipe with pumpkin or any other orange-flesh squash.

 Prepare:
5 minutes

 Cook:
10–15 minutes

 Servings:
4–6

ingredients

small wedge of butternut squash (about 85 g/3 oz)

85 g/3 oz baby pasta shapes

small knob of unsalted butter or polyunsaturated margarine

1 tsp olive oil

2 tbsp grated Cheddar cheese

Peel the butternut squash and scoop out the seeds. Chop the flesh into small cubes. Steam or cook the squash in enough unsalted boiling water just to cover for 10–15 minutes.

Drain the squash, reserving the cooking water, and blend until smooth. If necessary, thin with a little of the reserved cooking water.

Meanwhile, cook the pasta according to the packet instructions until it is tender. Drain and return to the pan. Add the butter, oil and cheese and stir until the pasta is thoroughly coated, then combine with the squash.

Serve lukewarm or store for up to 48 hours in the refrigerator or up to 8 weeks in the freezer.

my notes:

spring vegetable risotto

Rice is perfect for babies as the grains are soft, squashy and easy to eat. This recipe uses spring vegetables, but you can experiment with any others that you have to hand.

 Prepare: 5 minutes

 Cook: 35–40 minutes

 Servings: 6–8

ingredients

1 small leek, trimmed and finely chopped

1 small courgette, trimmed and finely chopped

small handful of frozen peas

1 tsp olive oil

small knob of unsalted butter or polyunsaturated margarine

85 g/3 oz risotto rice

350 ml/12 fl oz hot vegetable stock (see page 14) or water

½ tsp dried oregano

2 tbsp grated Cheddar cheese

Steam or cook the leek, courgette and peas in enough unsalted boiling water just to cover for 5–8 minutes. Drain. If wished, press the mixture through a sieve or mouli to remove the pea skins.

Meanwhile, heat the oil and butter in a saucepan until the butter has melted. Add the rice and stir until the grains are coated with the oil and butter.

Add the stock, a ladleful at a time, waiting until it has been absorbed before adding more. Simmer for 20 minutes, stirring frequently. Add the oregano, cheese and vegetable purée and cook, stirring, for a further 5–10 minutes, until the liquid has been absorbed and the rice is tender. Blend until smooth, adding a little water if it is too thick. For older babies, you can leave the mixture chunky.

Serve lukewarm or store for up to 48 hours in the refrigerator or up to 8 weeks in the freezer.

my notes:

....

....

....

chapter 3
meat

My baby's photo here

First meat baby tasted:

....

....

....

....

Baby's favourite meat/recipe:

....

....

....

....

Memorable moments:

....

....

....

....

beef & potato purée

Red meat is an excellent source of iron, which is an important nutrient for babies and toddlers. Babies are born with a store of iron that lasts for about 6 months, but after that they need to have iron in their diet.

 Prepare:
5 minutes

 Cook:
1½–2 hours

 Servings:
4–5

ingredients

50 g/1¾ oz red onion, finely chopped

200 g/7 oz stewing steak, trimmed of any fat and cubed

200 g/7 oz potatoes, peeled and cubed

250 ml/9 fl oz vegetable stock (see page 14) or water

pinch of dried thyme

Preheat the oven to 160°C/325°F/Gas Mark 3. Place all the ingredients in a flameproof casserole. Place over a medium heat and bring to the boil, then cover and transfer to the preheated oven to cook for 1½–2 hours, until the vegetables are tender and the meat starts to fall apart. Blend until smooth.

Serve lukewarm or store for up to 48 hours in the refrigerator or up to 8 weeks in the freezer.

my notes:

....

....

....

baby's first beef stew

Although foods like beans, pulses and dark green leafy vegetables contain iron, red meat is a more efficient source of iron as it contains it in a form that is more easily absorbed.

 Prepare: 10 minutes

 Cook: 1½–2 hours

 Servings: 5–6

ingredients

50 g/1¾ oz onion, finely chopped

1 garlic clove, crushed

150 g/5½ oz carrots, peeled and chopped

200 g/7 oz stewing steak, trimmed of any fat and cubed

200 g/7 oz potatoes, peeled and cubed

250 ml/9 fl oz vegetable stock (see page 14) or water

pinch of dried mixed herbs

Preheat the oven to 160°C/325°F/Gas Mark 3. Place all the ingredients in a flameproof casserole. Place over a medium heat and bring to the boil, then cover and transfer to the preheated oven to cook for 1½–2 hours, until the vegetables are tender and the meat starts to fall apart. Blend until smooth.

Serve lukewarm or store for up to 48 hours in the refrigerator or up to 8 weeks in the freezer.

my notes:

....

....

....

beef, sweet potato & spinach supper

Different coloured fruit and vegetables contain different nutrients and phytochemicals so giving your baby a variety is the best way to ensure they are getting all the nutrients they need.

 Prepare:
10 minutes

 Cook:
1½–2 hours

 Servings:
4

ingredients

250 g/9 oz sweet potato, peeled and cubed

100 g/3½ oz carrot, peeled and chopped

50 g/1¾ oz onion, finely chopped

200 g/7 oz stewing steak, trimmed of any fat and cubed

pinch of dried mixed herbs

300 ml/10 fl oz water

25 g/1 oz fresh spinach leaves, tough stalks removed

Preheat the oven to 160°C/325°F/Gas Mark 3. Place all the ingredients, except the spinach, in a flameproof casserole over a medium heat. Bring to the boil, then cover and transfer to the preheated oven for 1½–2 hours, until the vegetables are tender and the meat starts to fall apart.

Remove from the oven. Stir in the spinach, re-cover and simmer on the hob for 2–3 minutes to wilt the spinach. Blend until smooth.

Serve lukewarm or store for up to 48 hours in the refrigerator or up to 8 weeks in the freezer.

my notes:

....

....

....

my notes:

....

....

....

baby's first cottage pie

Cottage pie is a recipe that can be enjoyed by the whole family. This puréed version will get your baby used to the taste of family food but has a smooth texture that they will find more manageable at this stage.

 Prepare:
10 minutes

 Cook:
1½–2 hours

 Servings:
5–6

ingredients

50 g/1¾ oz onion, finely chopped

1 garlic clove, crushed

150 g/5½ oz carrots, peeled and chopped

200 g/7 oz stewing steak, trimmed of any fat and cubed

250 ml/9 fl oz vegetable stock (see page 14) or water

pinch of dried mixed herbs

mashed potatoes
200g/7 oz potatoes, peeled and cubed

2 tbsp full-fat milk

5 g/⅛ oz unsalted butter or polyunsaturated margarine

Preheat the oven to 160°C/325°F/Gas Mark 3. Place the onion, garlic, carrots, steak, stock and mixed herbs in a flameproof casserole. Place over a medium heat and bring to the boil, then cover and transfer to the preheated oven to cook for 1½–2 hours, until the vegetables are tender and the meat starts to fall apart.

Shortly before the stew is ready, cook the potatoes in a small saucepan of unsalted boiling water for 12–15 minutes, until tender. Drain and mash well with the milk and butter.

Blend the stew until smooth. Divide between 5–6 x 150-ml/5-fl oz ramekins or pie dishes and spoon or pipe the mashed potatoes on top.

Serve lukewarm or store for up to 48 hours in the refrigerator or up to 8 weeks in the freezer.

pasta bolognese

Canned tomatoes are a good source of the phytochemical lycopene. Although fresh tomatoes also contain this, the canning process breaks down the tomato's tough cell walls, making it easier for the body to absorb it.

 Prepare:
10 minutes

 Cook:
30–35 minutes

 Servings:
4–5

ingredients

1 tbsp olive oil

1 small onion, finely chopped

1 celery stick, trimmed and finely chopped

1 garlic clove, crushed

200 g/7 oz beef steak mince

2 tbsp tomato purée

400 g/14 oz canned chopped tomatoes

90 ml/3 fl oz vegetable stock (see page 14) or water

50 g/1¾ oz baby pasta shapes

Heat the oil in a frying pan over a medium heat and cook the onion, celery and garlic for 4–5 minutes, until starting to soften.

Add the beef mince and continue to cook for a further 4–5 minutes, until browned. Add the tomato purée and cook for 1 minute, stirring constantly.

Add the tomatoes and stock and bring to the boil. Cover and simmer for 20–25 minutes, until the beef is thoroughly cooked.

Meanwhile, cook the pasta according to the packet instructions until it is tender. Drain. Blend the bolognese sauce until smooth and stir in the pasta.

Serve lukewarm or store for up to 48 hours in the refrigerator or up to 8 weeks in the freezer.

my notes:
....
....
....

107

beany beef mash-up

Red meat is an excellent source of iron, which is needed by the body to make red blood cells. These transport oxygen around the body and are important for a healthy immune system.

 Prepare:
10 minutes

 Cook:
1½–2 hours

 Servings:
7–8

ingredients

50 g/1¾ oz onion, finely chopped

200 g/7 oz stewing steak, trimmed of any fat and cubed

1 celery stick, trimmed and chopped

70 g/2½ oz carrot, peeled and chopped

140 g/5 oz canned chopped tomatoes

175 ml/6 fl oz vegetable stock (see page 14) or water

70 g/2½ oz canned kidney beans in water, drained and rinsed

Preheat the oven to 160°C/325°F/Gas Mark 3. Place all the ingredients, except the kidney beans, in a flameproof casserole over a medium heat. Cover and bring to the boil, then transfer to the preheated oven for 1¼–1½ hours.

Remove from the oven. Stir in the kidney beans, re-cover and return to the oven for a further 15–30 minutes, until the vegetables are tender and the meat starts to fall apart. Blend until smooth.

Serve lukewarm or store for up to 48 hours in the refrigerator or up to 8 weeks in the freezer.

my notes:

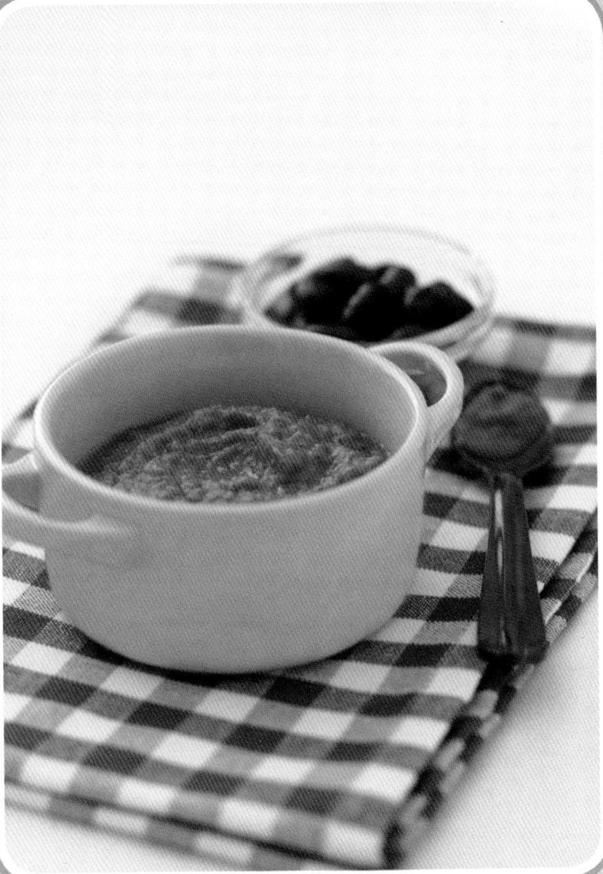

pork, apple & potato purée

Pork is a good source of B group vitamins, which help the body convert food into energy. They are also important for growth and the manufacture of red blood cells.

 Prepare: 10 minutes

 Cook: 1¼–1½ hours

 Servings: 6–7

ingredients

50 g/1¾ oz onion, finely chopped

70 g/2½ oz eating apple

140 g/5 oz potato, peeled and cubed

175 g/6 oz pork fillet, cubed

pinch of dried sage

275 ml/9 fl oz water

Preheat the oven to 160°C/325°F/Gas Mark 3. Place all the ingredients in a flameproof casserole dish over a medium heat. Cover and bring to the boil, then transfer to the preheated oven and cook for 1¼–1½ hours, until the vegetables and pork are completely tender. Blend until smooth.

Serve lukewarm or store for up to 48 hours in the refrigerator or up to 8 weeks in the freezer.

my notes:

....

....

....

creamy chicken & pineapple

This creamy purée is quick and easy to prepare. For older babies, it would make a perfect sandwich filling or could be served as a dip with fingers of toast. For a no-cook version, use leftover roast chicken.

 Prepare:
5 minutes

 Cook:
12–15 minutes

 Servings:
2

ingredients

1 tsp olive oil

55 g/2 oz skinless, boneless chicken breast, chopped

4 tbsp full-fat cream cheese

1 tbsp full-fat natural yogurt

slice of prepared fresh pineapple, diced

Heat the oil in a frying pan. Add the chicken and cook, stirring occasionally, for 12–15 minutes, until lightly browned. Leave to cool.

Blend the chicken to a smooth purée with the cream cheese, yogurt and pineapple.

Serve lukewarm or store for up to 48 hours in the refrigerator. Do not freeze.

my notes:

....

....

....

chicken, sweet potato & apple mash-up

Babies can sometimes be put off by the dry texture of chicken, so mixing it with vegetables in a soft purée is a good way of introducing it to your little one's diet. For older babies, you can leave the mixture chunky.

 Prepare: 10 minutes

 Cook: 25 minutes

 Servings: 2–3

ingredients

2 tsp olive oil

25 g/1 oz leek, finely chopped

55 g/2 oz skinless, boneless chicken breast, finely chopped

25 g/1 oz button mushrooms, finely chopped

25 g/1 oz potato or sweet potato, peeled and diced

½ small eating apple, peeled, cored and chopped

150 ml/5 fl oz vegetable stock (see page 14) or water

Heat the oil in a small saucepan over a medium heat. Add the leek and chicken and cook, stirring occasionally, for 8–10 minutes, until the leek is tender and the chicken is cooked through but not browned.

Add the mushrooms, potato and apple. Pour in the stock, cover and simmer gently for about 15 minutes, until the vegetables are tender. Blend until smooth.

Serve lukewarm or store for up to 48 hours in the refrigerator or up to 8 weeks in the freezer.

my notes:

....

....

....

my notes:

....

....

....

my notes:

....

....

....

super sweet & sour noodles

During the weaning process, it is important to introduce your baby to a variety of textures and flavours. Stir-fries are a good way to do this, but don't add soy sauce because it is too salty.

 Prepare:
10 minutes

 Cook:
30–35 minutes

 Servings:
5–6

ingredients

100 g/3½ oz dried fine egg noodles

1 tsp vegetable oil

50 g/1¾ oz onion, finely chopped

50 g/1¾ oz red pepper, deseeded and chopped

50 g/1¾ oz carrot, peeled and chopped

200 g/7 oz skinless, boneless chicken breast, cubed

1 tbsp tomato purée

85 g/3 oz canned pineapple chunks in juice (drained weight), plus 200 ml/7 fl oz juice from the can

Cook the noodles according to the packet instructions. Drain, then cover and keep warm.

Heat the oil in a saucepan over a medium–high heat and cook the onion, red pepper, carrot and chicken for 4–5 minutes, stirring frequently. Add the tomato purée and cook for 1 minute, stirring constantly.

Add the pineapple juice, cover and simmer for 15 minutes. Add the pineapple chunks, re-cover and cook for a further 5 minutes, making sure that the chicken is thoroughly cooked.

Snip the noodles into short lengths with scissors or chop to a size that is manageable for your baby. Blend the chicken mixture until smooth, then stir in the noodles.

Serve lukewarm or store for up to 48 hours in the refrigerator or up to 8 weeks in the freezer.

chicken, mushroom & sweetcorn pasta

Chicken is a good source of protein, which is needed for growth and development. It also provides group B vitamins and the mineral zinc, which is important for a healthy immune system.

 Prepare: 5 minutes

 Cook: 20–25 minutes

 Servings: 2

ingredients

15 g/½ oz onion, finely chopped

25 g/1 oz mushrooms, sliced

100 g/3½ oz skinless, boneless chicken breast, cubed

35 g/1¼ oz sweetcorn kernels, canned in water and drained, or frozen

125 ml/4 fl oz full-fat milk

25 g/1 oz baby pasta shapes

Place all the ingredients, except the pasta, in a saucepan. Cover and simmer gently for 15 minutes, stirring occasionally, until the chicken is thoroughly cooked. Blend until smooth. If wished, press the mixture through a sieve or mouli to remove the sweetcorn skins.

Meanwhile, cook the pasta according to the packet instructions until it is tender. Drain well. Stir the pasta into the chicken purée.

Serve lukewarm or store for up to 48 hours in the refrigerator. Do not freeze.

my notes:

chicken, cauliflower & coconut curry

It's important to introduce babies to a range of flavours so don't be nervous about giving them curry, just choose a mild curry powder. Coconut milk is high in saturated fat so make this an occasional treat.

 Prepare:
10 minutes

 Cook:
25 minutes

 Servings:
5–6

ingredients

1 tbsp vegetable oil

35 g/1¼ oz onion, finely chopped

1 garlic clove, crushed

175 g/6 oz skinless, boneless chicken breast, cubed

1 tsp mild curry powder

125 g/4½ oz cauliflower, trimmed and cut into small florets

200 ml/7 fl oz canned coconut milk

100 g/3½ oz frozen peas

Heat the oil in a saucepan over a medium heat and cook the onion, garlic and chicken for 4–5 minutes. Add the curry powder and continue cooking for a further minute, stirring constantly.

Add the cauliflower and coconut milk, cover and simmer for 12–15 minutes. Add the peas, stir and re-cover. Cook for a further 5 minutes.

Blend until smooth. If wished, press the mixture through a sieve or mouli to remove the pea skins.

Serve lukewarm or store for up to 48 hours in the refrigerator or up to 8 weeks in the freezer.

my notes:

my notes:

....

....

....

smashing sunday roast

There's no reason why your baby has to miss out when the rest of the family is having Sunday dinner. This mini roast can be cooked alongside the main roast and uses a single baking tray.

 Prepare:
5 minutes

 Cook:
25–30 minutes

 Servings:
3–4

ingredients

235 g/8½ oz skinless, boneless chicken breast

100 g/3½ oz carrot, peeled and cut into chunks

125 g/4½ oz parsnip, peeled and cut into chunks

40 g/1½ oz red onion, cut into wedges

1 tsp olive oil

100 ml/3½ fl oz full-fat milk

Preheat the oven to 200°C/400°F/Gas Mark 6. Line a small baking tray with baking paper.

Place the chicken, carrot, parsnip and onion on the prepared baking tray. Drizzle over the oil and toss everything to coat well.

Transfer to the preheated oven and cook for 25–30 minutes, until the chicken is tender and the juices run clear when a skewer is inserted into the thickest part of the meat.

Warm the milk gently, then blend with the roasted chicken and vegetables until smooth.

Serve lukewarm or store for up to 48 hours in the refrigerator or up to 8 weeks in the freezer.

tip
You can use the same weight of leftover roast chicken in this recipe – simply blend with the milk and roasted vegetables.

creamy turkey purée with pasta

Turkey is a good source of lean protein, as well as the group B vitamins niacin and B6, which are needed for a healthy nervous system. It also provides phosphorus, which is important for strong bones.

 Prepare:
5 minutes

 Cook:
20–25 minutes

 Servings:
5–6

ingredients

1 tsp vegetable oil

25 g/1 oz onion, finely chopped

100 g/3½ oz carrot, peeled and chopped

150 g/5½ oz turkey escalope, cubed

200 ml/7 fl oz full-fat milk

85 g/3 oz green beans, trimmed and cut into short lengths

50 g/1¾ oz baby pasta shapes

Heat the oil in a saucepan and cook the onion and carrot for 2–3 minutes, until softened. Add the turkey and milk, then bring to simmering point. Cover and cook gently for 10–12 minutes.

Add the green beans and cook for a further 2–3 minutes, until the turkey is thoroughly cooked and the vegetables are tender.

Meanwhile, cook the pasta according to the packet instructions until it is tender. Drain well. Blend the turkey mixture until smooth, then stir in the pasta.

Serve lukewarm or store for up to 48 hours in the refrigerator or up to 8 weeks in the freezer.

my notes:

....

....

....

turkey tagine with couscous

Herbs and spices, such as cinnamon, can be used to add flavour and interest to baby food without the need for salt. Although food without salt may taste bland to you, your baby won't miss it.

 Prepare:
10 minutes

 Cook:
30–35 minutes

 Servings:
4–5

ingredients

1 tsp vegetable oil

35 g/1¼ oz onion, finely chopped

1 garlic clove, crushed

100 g/3½ oz carrot, peeled and finely chopped

125 g/4½ oz turkey escalope, cubed

¼ tsp ground cinnamon (optional)

1 tsp mild curry powder

1 tbsp tomato purée

300 ml/10 fl oz vegetable stock (see page 14) or water

50 g/1¾ oz couscous

Heat the oil in a saucepan over a medium heat and cook the onion, garlic, carrot and turkey for 4–5 minutes, stirring occasionally.

Add the cinnamon (if using), curry powder and tomato purée. Cook for a further minute, stirring constantly. Add the stock and cook for 15–20 minutes, stirring occasionally, until the turkey is thoroughly cooked.

Blend until smooth. Stir in the couscous and cook gently for 1 minute. Remove from the heat, cover and leave to stand for 10 minutes, stirring occasionally.

Serve lukewarm or store for up to 48 hours in the refrigerator or up to 8 weeks in the freezer.

tip
Some babies can be sensitive to cinnamon so, if you aren't sure, leave it out.

my notes:

....
....
....

127

turkey & sweetcorn mash-up

Turkey is a good source of protein, which provides the building blocks for the body's growth and repair. As it is low in fat, turkey can sometimes be dry and is best served with a sauce or vegetable purée.

 Prepare:
5 minutes

 Cook:
20 minutes

 Servings:
6–7

ingredients

175 g/6 oz potatoes, peeled and cubed

115 g/4 oz carrot, peeled and cubed

150 g/5½ oz turkey escalope, cubed

85 g/3 oz sweetcorn kernels, canned in water and drained, or frozen

200 ml/7 fl oz full-fat milk

Place all the ingredients in a saucepan over a medium heat, cover and bring to simmering point.

Cook gently for 20 minutes, until the turkey is thoroughly cooked and the vegetables are tender. Blend until smooth. If wished, press the mixture through a sieve or mouli to remove the sweetcorn skins.

Serve lukewarm or store for up to 48 hours in the refrigerator or up to 8 weeks in the freezer.

my notes:

tasty turkey rice

Basmati rice has a lower glycaemic index than other varieties of rice. It's good to introduce your baby to a variety of grains during the weaning process so try couscous, polenta and quinoa as well.

 Prepare:
5 minutes

 Cook:
30 minutes

 Servings:
5–6

ingredients

40 g/1½ oz onion, finely chopped

150 g/5½ oz turkey escalope, cubed

100 g/3½ oz carrot, peeled and finely chopped

400 ml/14 fl oz vegetable stock (see page 14) or water

50 g/1¾ oz basmati rice, washed

70 g/2½ oz frozen broad beans

70 g/2½ oz frozen peas

Place the onion, turkey, carrot and stock in a saucepan over a medium heat. Cover and simmer for 15 minutes.

Stir in the rice, broad beans and peas and cook for a further 15 minutes, until the turkey is thoroughly cooked and the rice and vegetables are tender.

Blend until smooth. If wished, press the mixture through a sieve or mouli to remove the broad bean and pea skins.

Serve lukewarm or store for up to 48 hours in the refrigerator or up to 8 weeks in the freezer.

my notes:

....
....
....

sweet potato, turkey & cranberry supper

Adding fresh or dried fruit, such as cranberries or dried apricots, to savoury dishes helps to boost flavour, interest and texture. It also provides the antioxidant vitamin C.

Prepare:
5 minutes

Cook:
20–30 minutes

Servings:
6–7

ingredients

225 g/8 oz sweet potato, peeled and cubed

150 g/5½ oz turkey escalope, cubed

40 g/1½ oz onion, finely chopped

300 ml/10 fl oz vegetable stock (see page 14) or water

pinch of dried sage

100 g/3½ oz green beans, trimmed and cut into short lengths

50 g/1¾ oz fresh cranberries

Place the sweet potato, turkey, onion, stock and sage in a saucepan over a medium heat. Cover and bring to simmering point, then cook gently for 15–20 minutes.

Add the green beans and cranberries and cook for a further 5–10 minutes, until the turkey is thoroughly cooked and the vegetables are tender. Blend until smooth.

Serve lukewarm or store for up to 48 hours in the refrigerator or up to 8 weeks in the freezer.

my notes:

....

....

....

chapter 4
fish

My baby's photo here

First fish baby tasted:

....

....

....

....

Baby's favourite fish/recipe:

....

....

....

....

Memorable moments:

....

....

....

....

my notes:
....
....
....

sweet pea & salmon supper

Salmon is an excellent source of protein and healthy omega-3 fats. Salmon also provides group B vitamins, which are needed for making red blood cells and for a healthy nervous system.

 Prepare:
10 minutes

 Cook:
15–20 minutes

 Servings:
4

ingredients

175 g/6 oz skinless, boneless salmon fillet

small knob of unsalted butter or polyunsaturated margarine

175 g/6 oz potatoes, peeled and cubed

85 g/3 oz carrot, peeled and cubed

150 ml/5 fl oz full-fat milk

85 g/3 oz frozen peas

40 g/1½ oz Cheddar cheese, grated

Preheat the oven to 180°C/350°F/Gas Mark 4. Place the salmon in the centre of a square of foil. Top with the butter and loosely gather the foil. Place on a baking tray and cook in the preheated oven for 10–15 minutes, until the fish is opaque and flakes easily. Remove from the oven, flake and check for any bones.

Meanwhile, place the potatoes, carrot and milk in a small saucepan over a medium heat. Cover and simmer gently for 10–12 minutes, until the vegetables are almost tender. Add the peas and cook for a further 2–3 minutes.

Add the cooked fish to the vegetable mixture and blend until smooth. If wished, pass the mixture through a sieve or mouli to remove the pea skins. Stir in the cheese and mix with a fork until it has melted.

Serve lukewarm or store for up to 48 hours in the refrigerator or up to 8 weeks in the freezer.

creamy salmon pasta

Oily fish, such as salmon and tuna, is rich in omega-3 fatty acids, which are important for brain development. This simple recipe is a tasty way to introduce your baby to salmon.

 Prepare:
10 minutes

 Cook:
15 minutes

 Servings:
2

ingredients

40 g/1½ oz baby pasta shapes

25 g/1 oz broccoli florets

1 tsp olive oil

small knob of unsalted butter or polyunsaturated margarine

½ small leek, trimmed and finely chopped

140 g/5 oz skinless, boneless salmon fillet, cubed

2 tbsp full-fat cream cheese with garlic and herbs

1–1½ tbsp full-fat milk

Cook the pasta according to the packet instructions until it is tender. Steam or cook the broccoli in enough unsalted boiling water just to cover for 8–10 minutes, until tender.

Meanwhile, heat the oil and butter in a small frying pan over a medium heat, then add the leek and cook for 7 minutes, or until softened. Add the salmon and cook for 2 minutes, or until the salmon is just cooked and flakes apart easily. Check for any bones. Stir in the cream cheese and milk and heat through.

Drain the pasta and broccoli. Add the broccoli to the frying pan and stir to combine. Blend the salmon mixture until smooth, then stir in the pasta.

Serve lukewarm or store for up to 48 hours in the refrigerator. Do not freeze.

my notes:

....

....

....

salmon & asparagus risotto

Asparagus has a strong flavour so it is probably best not to offer it as your baby's very first food, but it can certainly be introduced once they are enjoying other vegetables and fruit.

 Prepare:
10 minutes

 Cook:
20–25 minutes

 Servings:
4

ingredients

1 tsp olive oil

40 g/1½ oz onion, finely chopped

85 g/3 oz risotto rice

400 ml/14 fl oz hot vegetable stock (see page 14) or water

175 g/6 oz skinless, boneless salmon fillet, cubed

50 g/1¾ oz asparagus, trimmed and cut into short lengths

Heat the oil in a saucepan over a medium heat and cook the onion for 2–3 minutes, until it starts to soften.

Add the rice and cook for a further minute, stirring constantly. Add half the stock and cook for 8–10 minutes, stirring occasionally.

Add the salmon, asparagus and the remaining stock, cover and cook for a further 8–10 minutes, until the rice is tender and the salmon is just cooked and flakes apart easily. Check for any bones. Blend until smooth.

Serve lukewarm or store for up to 48 hours in the refrigerator or up to 8 weeks in the freezer.

my notes:

....

....

....

my notes:

....

....

....

salmon fish pie

Both salmon and carrots are healthy foods in their own rights, but when they are eaten together they become even healthier! The healthy fat in the salmon helps the body to absorb the beta-carotene from the carrots.

 Prepare:
10 minutes

 Cook:
25–30 minutes

 Servings:
2

ingredients

75 g/2¾ oz skinless, boneless salmon fillet

small knob of unsalted butter or polyunsaturated margarine

50 g/1¾ oz carrot, peeled and chopped

4 tbsp full-fat milk

15 g/½ oz fresh spinach leaves, tough stalks removed

2 tbsp full-fat cream cheese

mashed potatoes
100 g/3½ oz potato, peeled and cubed

1 tbsp full-fat milk

small knob of unsalted butter or polyunsaturated margarine

Preheat the oven to 180°C/350°F/Gas Mark 4. Place the salmon in the centre of a square of foil. Top with the butter and loosely gather the foil. Place on a baking tray and cook in the preheated oven for 10–15 minutes, until the fish is opaque and flakes easily. Remove from the oven, flake and check for any bones.

Put the carrot and milk in a small saucepan. Cover and simmer for 10–12 minutes. Add the spinach and cook for 1–2 minutes, until wilted. Stir in the cream cheese and salmon. Blend until smooth.

Meanwhile, cook the potato in a small saucepan of unsalted boiling water for 12–15 minutes, until tender. Drain and mash well with the milk and butter.

Divide the salmon mixture between 2 x 150-ml/5-fl oz ramekins and spoon or pipe the mashed potatoes on top.

Serve lukewarm or store for up to 48 hours in the refrigerator. Do not freeze.

143

scrummy salmon noodles

Omega-3 fats, found in oil-rich fish like salmon, are important for brain development but they also help to keep the heart and nervous system healthy. The noodles add texture and essential carbohydrates.

 Prepare:
10 minutes

 Cook:
20–25 minutes

 Servings:
3

ingredients

50 g/1¾ oz dried fine egg noodles

½ tsp vegetable oil

25 g/1 oz onion, finely chopped

25 g/1 oz red pepper, deseeded and diced

40 g/1½ oz button mushrooms, sliced

½ tbsp tomato purée

200 g/7 oz canned chopped tomatoes

85 g/3 oz skinless, boneless salmon fillet, cubed

Cook the noodles according to the packet instructions. Drain, then cover to keep warm.

Meanwhile, heat the oil in a saucepan over a medium heat and cook the onion for 2–3 minutes. Add the red pepper and mushrooms and cook for a further 3–4 minutes.

Add the tomato purée and cook for a further minute, stirring constantly. Add the tomatoes, cover and cook gently for 10 minutes.

Add the salmon and continue cooking for a further 5 minutes, until the fish flakes apart easily. Check for any bones. Blend until smooth.

Snip the noodles into short lengths with scissors or chop to a size that is manageable for your baby. Stir the noodles into the sauce.

Serve lukewarm or store for up to 48 hours in the refrigerator. Do not freeze.

my notes:

....

....

....

tomato & salmon sauce with pasta

A baby's brain triples in size in the first year of their life, which means it has a high need for essential fatty acids. The best source is oil-rich fish, like salmon, so try to give your baby oily fish at least once a week.

 Prepare:
10 minutes

 Cook:
30–35 minutes

 Servings:
4–6

ingredients

85 g/3 oz baby pasta shapes

175 g/6 oz skinless, boneless salmon fillet

small knob of unsalted butter or polyunsaturated margarine

70 g/2½ oz carrot, peeled and finely chopped

1 celery stick, trimmed and finely chopped

200 g/7 oz canned chopped tomatoes

pinch of dried thyme

4 tbsp water

Preheat the oven to 180°C/350°F/Gas Mark 4. Cook the pasta according to the packet instructions until it is tender. Drain well, then cover to keep warm.

Meanwhile, place the salmon in the centre of a square of foil. Top with the butter and loosely gather the foil. Place on a baking tray and cook in the preheated oven for 10–12 minutes, until the fish is opaque and flakes easily. Remove from the oven, flake and check for any bones.

Place the carrot, celery, tomatoes, thyme and water in a small saucepan over a medium heat. Cover and simmer for 15–20 minutes, until the vegetables are tender. Add the cooked salmon to the tomato mixture and blend until smooth. Stir in the cooked pasta.

Serve lukewarm or store for up to 48 hours in the refrigerator or up to 8 weeks in the freezer.

my notes:

....

....

....

my notes:

....
....
....

cheesy tuna & sweetcorn pasta

Canned tuna contains less omega-3 fats than fresh tuna. However, canned tuna does contain plenty of other good nutrients, including protein and B group vitamins. Choose tuna canned in spring water or oil, rather than brine.

 Prepare:
10 minutes

 Cook:
10–15 minutes

 Servings:
5–6

ingredients

85 g/3 oz baby
pasta shapes

15 g/½ oz unsalted
butter or polyunsaturated
margarine

40 g/1½ oz onion,
finely chopped

1 tbsp plain flour

150 ml/5 fl oz full-fat milk

50 g/1¾ oz mature
Cheddar cheese, grated

150 g/5½ oz tuna in spring
water or oil, drained

70 g/2½ oz sweetcorn
kernels, canned in water
and drained, or frozen

Cook the pasta according to the packet instructions until it is tender. Drain well, then cover and keep warm.

Meanwhile, melt the butter in a saucepan over a medium heat and cook the onion for 2–3 minutes, until starting to soften. Add the flour and cook for 1 minute, stirring constantly. Gradually add the milk, stirring after each addition. When all the milk has been added, bring to the boil and cook for 1 minute.

Add the cheese, tuna and sweetcorn and stir until the cheese has melted. Blend until smooth. If wished, press the mixture through a sieve or mouli to remove the sweetcorn skins. Stir in the cooked pasta.

Serve lukewarm or store for up to 48 hours in the refrigerator or up to 8 weeks in the freezer.

no-cook avocado & tuna mash-up

Avocados are packed with important nutrients, including vitamins C, E and B6, iron and magnesium. For older babies, you can serve this recipe spread on toast or an oatcake. It is also good when served as a filling in a jacket potato.

 Prepare: 5 minutes

 Cook: 0 minutes

 Servings: 1

ingredients

40 g/1½ oz canned tuna in spring water

½ ripe avocado

1 tbsp mayonnaise (not home-made)

Drain the tuna and flake into a small bowl. Remove the stone from the avocado and scoop out the flesh with a spoon.

Add the avocado and mayonnaise to the tuna and mash well with a fork until smooth.

Serve immediately. Do not refrigerate or freeze.

my notes:

....
....
....

simple sole with potato & spinach

Sole is a good choice for the early stages of weaning as it has a delicate, soft texture and a mild flavour. Like all white fish, it is a good source of protein, group B vitamins and the mineral selenium.

 Prepare:
10 minutes

 Cook:
20–25 minutes

 Servings:
4

ingredients

175 ml/6 fl oz full-fat milk

175 g/6 oz potatoes, peeled and cubed

85 g/3 oz carrot, peeled and chopped

150 g/5½ oz skinless, boneless sole fillet, cubed

50 g/1¾ oz fresh spinach leaves, tough stalks removed

finely grated rind of ½ lemon

Pour the milk into a medium saucepan and add the potatoes and carrot. Cover and simmer gently for 12–15 minutes.

Add the sole and continue to cook for a further 4–5 minutes. Stir in the spinach and cook for 2–3 minutes, until the spinach is wilted and the fish is just cooked and flakes easily. Check for any bones. Add the lemon rind, then blend until smooth.

Serve lukewarm or store for up to 48 hours in the refrigerator or up to 8 weeks in the freezer.

my notes:

....

....

....

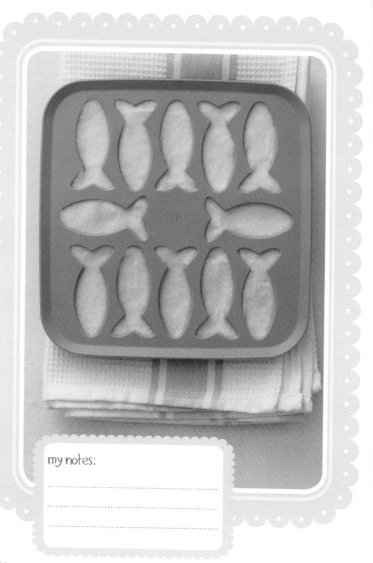

my notes:

....

....

....

creamy sole chowder

Sole contains the mineral selenium, which is important for healthy hair and nails. Selenium also helps to create a healthy immune system and to protect against heart disease.

 Prepare: 10 minutes

 Cook: 25–30 minutes

 Servings: 5–6

ingredients

15 g/½ oz unsalted butter or polyunsaturated margarine

40 g/1½ oz onion, finely chopped

1 small celery stick, trimmed and finely chopped

1 tbsp plain flour

150 ml/5 fl oz full-fat milk

150 g/5½ oz potatoes, peeled and cubed

150 g/5½ oz skinless, boneless lemon sole fillet, cubed

125 g/4½ oz sweetcorn kernels, canned in water and drained, or frozen

Melt the butter in a saucepan over a medium heat and cook the onion and celery for 2–3 minutes, until starting to soften.

Add the flour and cook for 1 minute, stirring constantly. Gradually add the milk, stirring after each addition. When all the milk has been added, bring to the boil and cook for 1 minute.

Add the potatoes and cook for 12–15 minutes. Add the sole and sweetcorn and cook gently for 5–6 minutes, until the fish is just cooked and flakes apart easily. Check for any bones.

Blend until smooth. If wished, press the mixture through a sieve or mouli to remove the sweetcorn skins.

Serve lukewarm or store for up to 48 hours in the refrigerator or up to 8 weeks in the freezer.

oven-baked sole with tomatoes & potatoes

Sole is very low in fat so, in the early stages of weaning, it is best combined with fatty ingredients, such as milk, to make a sauce. Cherry tomatoes boost the nutritional value of the dish by adding vitamins C and B6.

 Prepare:
10 minutes

 Cook:
25–30 minutes

 Servings:
4

ingredients

175 g/6 oz skinless, boneless lemon sole fillet

85 g/3 oz cherry tomatoes, halved

150 g/5½ oz new potatoes, scrubbed and cubed

90 ml/3 fl oz full-fat milk

Preheat the oven to 180°C/350°F/Gas Mark 4. Place the sole, tomatoes, potatoes and milk in a small ovenproof dish. Cover with foil and bake in the preheated oven for 25–30 minutes, until the potatoes are tender and the fish flakes apart easily. Check for any bones. Blend until smooth.

Serve lukewarm or store for up to 48 hours in the refrigerator or up to 8 weeks in the freezer.

my notes:

156

white fish, broccoli & courgette combo

Broccoli is a great source of vitamin C and the B vitamin folate, as well as providing the minerals iron and potassium. It is best not to peel the courgette as many of its nutrients are in the skin.

 Prepare:
10 minutes

 Cook:
10–12 minutes

 Servings:
4

ingredients

25 g/1 oz onion, finely chopped

140 g/5 oz skinless, boneless halibut fillet, cubed

175 ml/6 fl oz full-fat milk

100 g/3½ oz broccoli, cut into small florets

70 g/2½ oz courgette, trimmed and finely cubed

Place all the ingredients in a saucepan over a medium heat, cover and simmer gently for 10–12 minutes, until the vegetables are tender and the fish flakes apart easily. Check for any bones. Blend until smooth.

Serve lukewarm or store for up to 48 hours in the refrigerator or up to 8 weeks in the freezer.

my notes:

....

....

....

cheesy potato & halibut mash

Frozen peas are a great ingredient, as they are frozen within hours of being picked so the vitamins remain preserved. The vitamin C from the peas will also facilitate the absorption of iron from the fish.

 Prepare:
10 minutes

 Cook:
10–12 minutes

 Servings:
4

ingredients

140 g/5 oz skinless, boneless halibut fillet, cubed

150 ml/5 fl oz full-fat milk

200 g/7 oz potatoes, peeled and cubed

100 g/3½ oz frozen peas

25 g/1 oz mature Cheddar cheese, grated

Place all the ingredients, except the cheese, in a saucepan over a medium heat. Cover and simmer gently for 10–12 minutes, until the vegetables are tender and the fish flakes apart easily. Check for any bones.

Blend until smooth. If wished, press the mixture through a sieve or mouli to remove the pea skins. Stir in the cheese.

Serve lukewarm or store for up to 48 hours in the refrigerator or up to 8 weeks in the freezer.

my notes:

....

....

....

hearty halibut & tomato pasta

This tangy tomato sauce is the perfect accompaniment to pasta. Halibut is a good source of vitamin B12, which is important for the manufacture of red blood cells and a healthy immune system.

 Prepare: 10 minutes

 Cook: 35–40 minutes

 Servings: 6–7

ingredients

50 g/1¾ oz baby pasta shapes

1 tbsp olive oil

40 g/1½ oz onion, finely chopped

2 small celery sticks, trimmed and finely chopped

100 g/3½ oz courgette, trimmed and cut into small cubes

2 tbsp tomato purée

400 g/14 oz canned chopped tomatoes

90 ml/3 fl oz vegetable stock (see page 14) or water

140 g/5 oz skinless, boneless halibut fillet, cubed

Cook the pasta according to the packet instructions until it is tender. Drain well, then cover to keep warm.

Meanwhile, heat the oil in a frying pan over a medium heat and cook the onion, celery and courgette for 4–5 minutes, until starting to soften.

Add the tomato purée and cook for 1 minute, stirring constantly. Add the tomatoes and stock and bring to the boil. Cover and simmer for 15–20 minutes.

Add the halibut, cover and cook gently for a further 5 minutes, until the fish flakes apart easily. Check for any bones.

Blend the sauce until smooth. Stir the pasta into the sauce.

Serve lukewarm or store for up to 48 hours in the refrigerator or up to 8 weeks in the freezer.

my notes:
....
....
....

163

grilled halibut with mango salsa

The mango salsa gives this recipe an interesting, fruity twist. Not only will babies love the sweet taste, but it also provides the vital vitamins C, E and B6 at the same time.

 Prepare: 10 minutes

 Cook: 4–5 minutes

 Servings: 1

ingredients

40 g/1½ oz skinless, boneless halibut fillet, cubed

½ ripe avocado, peeled, stoned and cubed

50 g/1¾ oz ripe mango, peeled, stoned and cubed

25 g/1 oz cherry tomatoes, quartered

1 tsp chopped fresh basil leaves

2 tbsp orange juice

Preheat the grill to medium. Cook the halibut under the preheated grill for 4–5 minutes, until it flakes apart easily. Check for any bones.

Blend the cooked halibut with the avocado, mango, tomatoes, basil and orange juice until smooth.

Serve immediately. Do not refrigerate or freeze.

my notes:

....

....

....

easy-peasy flounder & potato mash

Adding a hint of lemon to this dish provides a delicate flavour without the need to add any salt. You could also try adding some finely chopped chives or basil to boost the flavour even more.

 Prepare:
10 minutes

 Cook:
25–30 minutes

 Servings:
5–6

ingredients

175 g/6 oz skinless, boneless flounder or plaice fillet

175 ml/6 fl oz full-fat milk

200 g/7 oz potatoes, peeled and cubed

finely grated rind of ½ lemon

Preheat the oven to 180°C/350°F/Gas Mark 4. Place all the ingredients in a shallow ovenproof dish and cover loosely with foil. Bake in the preheated oven for 25–30 minutes, until the potatoes are tender and the fish flakes apart easily. Check for any bones. Blend until smooth.

Serve lukewarm or store for up to 48 hours in the refrigerator or up to 8 weeks in the freezer.

my notes:

....

....

....

flounder, butternut squash & carrot combo

Flounder is quick to cook, making it perfect for busy parents on the go! It also has a mild flavour and delicate texture so is a fantastically versatile ingredient and ideal as a weaning food.

Prepare:
10 minutes

Cook:
20 minutes

Servings:
4

ingredients

40 g/1½ oz red onion, finely chopped

100 g/3½ oz carrot, peeled and finely chopped

150 g/5½ oz butternut squash, peeled, deseeded and cubed

175 ml/6 fl oz full-fat milk

140 g/5 oz boneless, skinless flounder or plaice fillet, cubed

Place all the ingredients, except the flounder, in a saucepan over a medium heat. Cover and simmer for 15 minutes.

Add the flounder, cover and cook gently for a further 5 minutes, until the vegetables are tender and the fish flakes apart easily. Check for any bones. Blend until smooth.

Serve lukewarm or store for up to 48 hours in the refrigerator or up to 8 weeks in the freezer.

my notes:

....

....

....

feel-good fish with tomato, sweetcorn & peas

This is a great standby recipe as it can be made from items in your store cupboard or freezer. If you use canned sweetcorn, choose a variety without any added salt or sugar.

 Prepare:
10 minutes

 Cook:
20 minutes

 Servings:
4

ingredients

1 tsp vegetable oil

1 garlic clove, crushed

40 g/1½ oz onion, finely chopped

200 g/7 oz canned chopped tomatoes

1–2 tbsp water

140 g/5 oz skinless, boneless flounder or plaice fillet, cubed

70 g/2½ oz sweetcorn kernels, canned in water and drained, or frozen

70 g/2½ oz frozen peas

Heat the oil in a saucepan over a medium heat and cook the garlic and onion for 3–4 minutes, until starting to soften.

Add the tomatoes and water. Cover and simmer for 10 minutes.

Add the fish, sweetcorn and peas. Cover and cook gently for a further 5–6 minutes, until the fish flakes apart easily. Check for any bones.

Blend until smooth. If wished, press the mixture through a sieve or mouli to remove the sweetcorn and pea skins.

Serve lukewarm or store for up to 48 hours in the refrigerator or up to 8 weeks in the freezer.

my notes:

....

....

....

cheesy flounder with green vegetables

As white fish is extremely low in fat, it is important to ensure your baby is getting enough calories. This recipe combines fish with cheese, which contains more fat, or you could also try avocado.

 Prepare:
10 minutes

 Cook:
20–25 minutes

 Servings:
4–5

ingredients

25 g/1 oz onion, finely chopped

200 g/7 oz courgette, trimmed and finely chopped

115 g/4 oz broccoli florets

200 ml/7 fl oz full-fat milk

150 g/5½ oz skinless, boneless flounder or plaice fillet, cubed

40 g/1½ oz mature Cheddar cheese, grated

Place the onion, courgette, broccoli and milk in a saucepan. Cover and bring to a gentle simmer for about 12–14 minutes.

Add the flounder, cover and continue cooking gently for a further 6–7 minutes, until the fish flakes apart easily. Check for any bones, then stir in the cheese until it melts. Blend until smooth.

Serve lukewarm or store for up to 48 hours in the refrigerator or up to 8 weeks in the freezer.

my notes:

....

....

....

super-yummy fish & vegetable purée

Cauliflower is a good source of folate, potassium and vitamin C, while the white fish is abundant in iodine, which is essential for the good functioning of the thyroid gland.

 Prepare:
10 minutes

 Cook:
15–20 minutes

 Servings:
4–5

ingredients

100 g/3½ oz carrot, peeled and cubed

100 g/3½ oz cauliflower, trimmed and cut into small florets

175 g/6 oz sweet potato, peeled and cubed

200 ml/7 fl oz water

140 g/5 oz skinless, boneless flounder or plaice fillet, cubed

Place all the ingredients, except the flounder, in a saucepan over a medium heat. Cover and simmer gently for 10–12 minutes.

Add the fish, cover and cook gently for a further 4–5 minutes, until it flakes apart easily. Check for any bones. Blend until smooth.

Serve lukewarm or store for up to 48 hours in the refrigerator or up to 8 weeks in the freezer.

my notes:

....

....

....

175